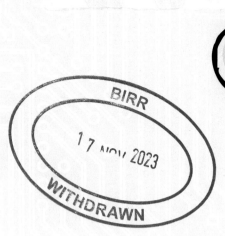

Get AHEAD in COMPUTING

The Science of COMPUTERS

Clive Gifford

WAYLAND

Published in paperback in 2016 by Wayland
Copyright © Wayland 2016

Wayland, an imprint of Hachette Children's Group
Part of Hodder & Stoughton
Carmelite House
50 Victoria Embankment
London EC4Y 0DZ

Commissioning Editor: Debbie Foy
Project Editor: Caroline West (Blue Dragonfly Ltd.)
Designer: Mark Latter (Blue Dragonfly Ltd.)

A catalogue record for this title is available
from the British Library.

ISBN: 978 0 7502 9215 3
Library eBook ISBN: 978 0 7502 9214 6
Dewey number: 004-dc23

MIX
Paper from
responsible sources
FSC® C104740

Printed in China

An Hachette UK company
www.hachette.co.uk
www.hachettechildrens.co.uk

All images courtesy of Shutterstock except: p6 Bletchley Park
Trust/Science & Society Picture Library; p7 (bottom right) Science
Museum/Science & Society Picture Library; and p29 (centre right)
IStockphoto/Staffan Andersson.

Disclaimer: The website addresses (URLs) included in this book were
valid at the time of going to press. However, because of the nature of
the Internet, it is possible that some addresses may have changed,
or sites may have changed or closed down since publication. While
the author and publisher regret any inconvenience this may cause the
readers, no responsibility for any such changes can be accepted by
either the author or the publisher.

Note to reader: Words highlighted in bold appear in the Glossary on
page 30. Answers to activities are on page 31.

Contents

A World of Computers

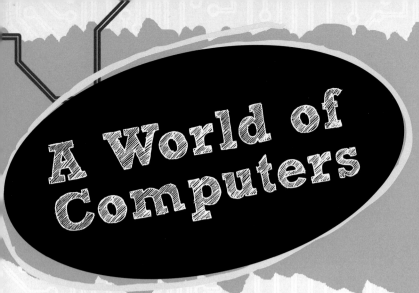

Computers are amazing machines. They are able to store, handle and retrieve information, which is known as data. Computers can be programmed in different ways to perform a huge variety of tasks.

Computers everywhere

Computer technology is found in the unlikeliest of places. Things that you don't think of as computers, such as microwave ovens, toasters, cameras and traffic lights, all have computer technology inside them and are **programmed** to perform a limited set of tasks. Other computers, such as laptops or tablets, can do lots of different jobs.

Desktop computers

Also known as PCs, these have a case and usually a separate screen. PCs are found in millions of homes, schools and offices.

Laptops

Also known as notebooks, these are portable computers with a battery inside for working away from home. Almost all laptops feature a solid keyboard for typing on.

In-car computers

These constantly check on the car's engine and other important parts. They can often adjust how the car performs, as well as warn drivers when there is a problem.

Washing machines

Did you know that the different types of wash performed by a washing machine are controlled by a small computer?

ATM machines

Bank machines give out cash when someone inserts a card or sends a mobile phone code; they are linked to computers inside the bank that keep track of the money.

Tablets

Slim, lightweight and battery-powered, these devices have a screen that you touch and swipe to read books, watch videos and many other things besides.

Smartphones

These mobile phones have real computing power inside their small cases. For example, you can check emails, view websites and play music.

TRUE STORY

Pump Up The Power Computers are getting faster and more powerful. For example, the latest Xbox 360 games console has more power than the flight computer that controlled the USA Space Shuttles on their 135 missions into space.

Games consoles

These are packed with computing power to run amazing, fast-moving games.

5

The Incredible Shrinking Computer

The first programmable computers were developed in the 1940s. Many were huge machines that filled whole rooms, but computer parts quickly got smaller, faster and more reliable.

Early computers

Early computers used hundreds or thousands of large electrical parts to act as switches and to store information. These often broke down.

ENIAC (Electronic Numerical Integrator And Computer) was one early computer used in the United States from 1946 to 1955. The longest period it worked without a part needing to be replaced in those ten years was just five days.

This picture shows the control panels of the Colossus Mark II from 1943, which was the world's first programmable computer.

ENIAC was almost the size of a basketball court. In 1995, 40 years after it was switched off, computing students managed to put all of ENIAC's functions on a single **silicon chip** that measured 7.5mm by 5.3mm – which is smaller than your fingernail.

The smallest silicon chips contain thousands of tiny circuits.

TRUE STORY

A Real Heavyweight The Sage computer was designed in the 1950s to track enemy aircraft. It was the world's heaviest computer system, weighing 227 tonnes — which is as much as 38 adult African elephants!

Some silicon chips are so small that ants can carry them.

Shrinking chips!

Engineers from the late 1950s onwards shrank the size of a computer's parts so that lots of them could fit on a tiny wafer of material. This integrated circuit, or silicon chip, could also be built more cheaply than traditional parts. Silicon chips also worked much faster and were more reliable.

COMPUTER Hero!

Charles Babbage tried to build the first computers in the 1820s and 1830s out of metal gears and other parts. Babbage didn't complete his 'engines', but was ahead of his time and worked out lots of the parts that would be needed in modern computers.

Charles Babbage

Here's the Hardware

The parts of a computer you can touch, such as the case, screen and insides, are called its hardware. But a computer with just hardware won't do a thing. It also needs the programs stored inside.

Operating systems

The collection of programs (or software) that controls how a computer works is called an **operating system** (OS). Android, for example, is a popular operating system for smartphones and tablets. Other programs work with the operating system to let you send emails, play games or do your homework, for example.

The Android robot

Plugged in

Extra pieces of hardware called **peripherals** can be attached to most computers. You can physically attach some of these using a cable. Other peripherals are wireless and work with the computer by sending and receiving signals carried by light or radio waves.

PC PORTS

The back of a PC has lots of sockets called ports that let you plug in different peripherals. You can see some of the most common ports here.

This picture shows the back of a computer without the plastic casing that surrounds the different ports.

1. Monitor
This port connects a monitor screen to a computer to display programs or images.

2. USB
USB (Universal Serial Bus) ports accept a range of different peripherals such as a USB mouse (see page 17) and a printer (see page 20).

3. Ethernet Port
This port takes a cable that connects a PC to a network of other computers.

4. Audio
Speakers and headphones are plugged into these ports to play sounds from the computer.

STRETCH YOURSELF

Find the Computer Port
Here are images of three different ports.

Can you work out what each port is used for by answering the following questions:

👉 Which port connects a USB mouse to a computer?

👉 Which port connects headphones to a computer?

👉 Which port is used for plugging in monitors?

a

b

c

Answers on page 31

Let's Look Inside

If you open up the desktop or tower case of a typical PC and peek inside, you'll find that nearly all computers have lots of similar parts.

CD/DVD drive
This box plays compact discs and DVDs on the computer or is used to load programs onto the machine.

PSU (Power Supply Unit)
A PSU takes electricity from a plug socket and supplies it to the rest of the computer.

Hard disk
This stores large amounts of data and programs (see page 14). Tablets and some laptops use memory chips instead of hard disks for storage.

Fan
A computer's parts can get hot, so a fan inside blows cooling air over them.

Cards
These cards are printed circuit boards that have electronic parts fitted to them to do a particular job. A sound card, for example, will generate and play all the sounds a computer can make.

Expansion slots
These are spare places for slotting extra cards into the computer.

MOTHERBOARD

A **motherboard** is a circuit board that contains connections to other parts of the computer. It features crucial parts such as two types of computer memory, RAM and ROM, and the CPU – which is the real brains of the computer.

1. CPU
(Central Processing Unit)
This is a powerful chip known as a microprocessor. The CPU does all the computer's calculations and also controls its other parts.

2. ROM
(Read Only Memory)
This cannot be changed by a user, but stores programs and information even when the computer is switched off. ROM also holds the instructions that are used to start a computer.

3. RAM
(Random Access Memory)
A computer uses silicon chips containing RAM as its temporary workspace for storing programs and data while it is working. RAM chips connect to the motherboard using these memory slots. When you turn off a computer, the RAM empties and the data is lost.

TRUE STORY

Let's Cool Off When working hard, some CPUs get hotter than boiling water (over 100°C), or they would do if they weren't fitted with a fan and **heatsink** to cool them down. A heatsink carries heat away from the CPU.

STAY SAFE!

Computers are powered by electricity, which can harm you if you are not careful. Follow these tips to stay safe:

1. Always unplug a computer before you move it.

2. Never yank a plug out of its socket by the wire. Pull it out gently holding the plastic casing.

3. Only ever hold the casing of a plug when you plug it into, or take it out of, a socket. Never touch the pins.

4. Never let water or any liquid get close to a computer.

Data and Circuits

Computers are useful because they can handle lots of information. They do this by breaking down the information into numbers that their electrical circuits can process quickly.

Ins and outs

All computers receive data from a source (known as input), which they store and work on (this is called processing) according to their programs. They output the results of their work in some way, such as displaying numbers on a screen or sending commands to a robot that the computer is controlling.

Input ➭ Processing ➭ Output

Storage

COMPUTER BRAIN

You perform just like a computer when you are given an addition sum to do. The input is hearing or reading the sum, the processing is adding up the numbers, and the output is saying the answer or writing it down.

Computers store and process all sorts of data, such as photographs and music, as long streams of **binary** numbers – just ones and zeros. A computer's chips are packed with electrical circuits and switches. The data flows round these circuits as patterns of tiny pulses of electrical signals, which represent the ones and zeros.

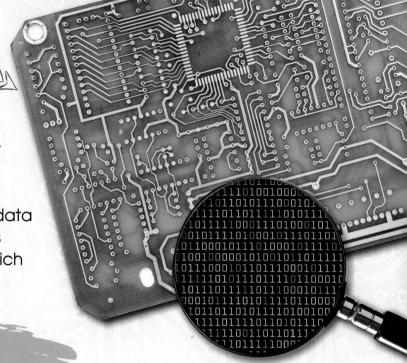

STRETCH YOURSELF

Build an Electrical Circuit
You can see how electricity flows through a circuit by making a simple electrical circuit and switch. Ask an adult to help you connect up a battery, a small light bulb, some electrical wire, a small piece of wood, two drawing pins and a paper clip in the same way as the diagram below.

Why is the paper clip so important?
The paper clip is the circuit switch. When you put it on the drawing pin, the circuit is completed, electricity flows from the battery around the whole circuit and lights up the bulb. Removing the paper clip breaks the circuit and switches off the bulb.

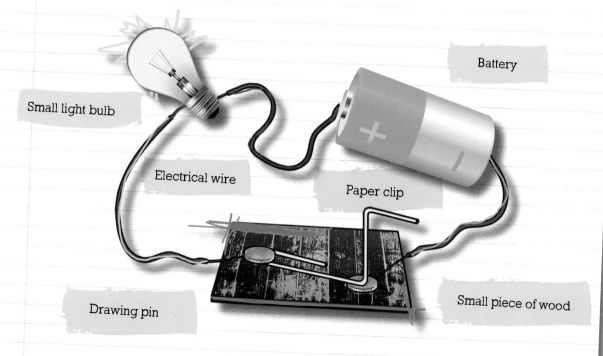

Small light bulb

Battery

Electrical wire

Paper clip

Drawing pin

Small piece of wood

Memory Matters

Do You Remember?

RAM
Random Access Memory

ROM
Read-Only Memory

(see page 11)

Computers use other types of memory besides the RAM and ROM found on their motherboards. These all play a role in storing programs or information.

Byte size

Memory is measured in bytes – lots of them. In a single **byte**, there are usually eight binary digits. A kilobyte is 1,000 or 1,024 bytes, but computers today work in megabytes and gigabytes. Each one of the following measures of memory is 1,000 times bigger than the last.

Spinning disks

Hard disks are found in many computers and also in digital recorders that record TV programmes. Hard disks can store hundreds of gigabytes on their spinning metal platters. In some hard disks, these platters spin round as fast as 200 times a second!

KB	MB	GB	TB
Kilobyte	Megabyte	Gigabyte	Terabyte
1,000 bytes	1,000,000 bytes	1,000,000,000 bytes	1,000,000,000,000 bytes

A single gigabyte (GB) of memory can hold over 8 billion binary numbers – that's more figures than the number of people on the planet. Many smartphones come with a built-in memory of 16GB or more.

Add more memory

You can easily increase a computer's storage abilities by plugging in external memory. This might be a memory card, which can be the size of a postage stamp or even smaller, or an external hard disk in its own case.

Back it up

Good computer users always make a regular backup (copy) of their files. You can store this backup on a pen drive, an external hard disk or a compact disc (CD). If there's a problem with your computer, then all your important files will still be safe and sound.

Another form of external memory is a pen drive. This plugs into a USB port and contains a small memory chip.

STRETCH YOURSELF

Sorting Data

Ask an adult to help you work out the size of some typical files on a computer using a computer's file manager program.

Write down the size of files holding a movie video, a music file and a document (such as a letter).

☞ Which was the biggest?

☞ Can you use a calculator to work out how many of each type of file would fit on the different memory devices below?

TRUE STORY

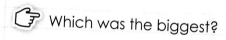

Heavy Hard Disk The first hard disk was built in 1956. The huge IBM 350 disk storage unit weighed almost 1,000kg and could only be moved by forklift truck. It held just 3.75 megabytes, which is a tiny fraction of the memory in today's mobile phones.

Memory card 2,000MB

CD-Rom 650MB

Hard disk 100,000MB

Input Devices: Keyboards and Mice

All computers need ways for you to enter commands or data. There are many different types of input device. The ones people use most often are a keyboard, mouse and trackpad.

Computer keyboards

A keyboard lets you type words and numbers into a computer to write an email or control a program. Each key is a switch. When you press a key down, it sends a signal to the computer to let it know it's been pressed.

A row of function keys (F1 to F12) calls up different options depending on the program you're using. Pressing F1 in many programs, for example, opens help information.

You press the arrow or cursor keys to move around the screen.

Some keyboards are made out of flexible plastic and can be rolled up and packed away.

This virtual keyboard is made of a grid of light beams projected onto a flat surface. You type by letting your fingers touch the light making up each key.

Computer mice

A mouse is a handy tool that lets you move a pointer called a **cursor** around the screen. Buttons on the mouse let you select options in a program. There is often a scroll wheel in between the buttons. You can use this to scroll (move) up or down the screen to look through a long document.

COMPUTER Hero!

Douglas Engelbart was an American computer engineer. In 1963, he built the first mouse out of wood with a single red button. Engelbart's mouse didn't catch on for 20 years, but since then over one billion have been sold.

Trackpads

Found on laptops, these flat pads use your finger to control the cursor on screen. A grid of electrical circuits underneath the pad detects the movement and turns it into electrical signals that are then sent back to the computer.

You can also get separate trackpads that work in the same way as integrated ones, but are designed for desktop computers rather than laptops.

More Input Devices: Touchscreens and Scanners

You don't always need a keyboard or mouse to send data or commands to a computer. Some computers and smartphones, for example, react to your voice or the touch of a screen.

Touchy feely screens

Tablets, many phones and some laptops have a touchscreen. When you press the screen or move your fingers across it, the device will perform different tasks, depending on the program you are using. For example, swiping the screen while reading an **e-book** can make the page turn, just like a real book.

Pinch and zoom

Some multi-touch screens recognise two touches at the same time. When two fingers touch the screen and move outwards, the computer zooms in on part of the screen to give you a close-up view. Moving your fingers together, which is called a pinch, does the opposite.

Scan that

Document scanners turn the writing and images on a piece of paper into data that a computer can store and use. Scanners are often used in offices, but you can also use them at home to copy pictures or photos.

Barcode scanners

A barcode is a pattern of black and white stripes on things you buy in shops. At the checkout, a special scanner can recognise an item from its code, compare this to the shop's database of items and call up the price.

Graphics tablets

A graphics tablet is like a larger, but more accurate, trackpad (see page 17), but you use a pen-shaped **stylus** instead of your fingertips. Designers, fashion designers and artists, as well as cartoon and movie animators, use graphics tablets and can select different colours, brush sizes and other effects. Graphics tablets are also used by architects to design buildings.

Output Devices

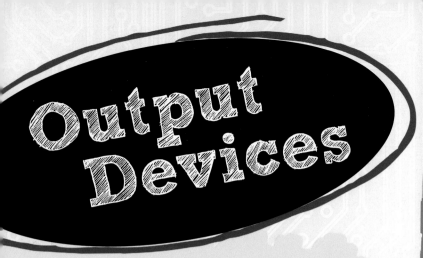

After running programs and processing data, a computer passes on the results of its work. This is called its output. Computer screens, printers and loudspeakers are all types of output device.

Print it out

A printer turns the computer's output into a hard copy on paper for you to read and keep. **Inkjet** printers, for example, allow people to print digital photos and documents from a computer in colour.

STRETCH YOURSELF

Print a Greetings Card
Ask an adult to help you design and print out a greetings card. Whatever computer and program you are using, set the paper to landscape (this means that the paper is wider than it is tall).

Put the main picture on the right half of the page, so that when you print it out you can fold the paper in half and finish the card.

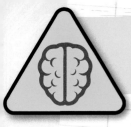

STRETCH YOURSELF

Can You Help Save the Planet?

Over 65 million plastic inkjet cartridges are sold in the United Kingdom each year. Most are thrown away when they're empty, but can take a long time to break down.

Your task is to find out some different ways to recycle these cartridges. Why not also ask your teacher to help you set up a cartridge-recycling box at school?

3D printing

Some printers can print actual objects. A three-dimensional (3D) design of the object is created on a computer. The design is then sent as a file to a 3D printer. This 'prints' a thin layer of the object using a material such as plastic or metal instead of ink. It carries on printing in layers until the whole object is complete.

The range of objects that have already been 3D-printed is amazing – from car parts and sculptures to smartphone cases and jewellery. Scientists are even working on how to print replacement teeth and other body parts!

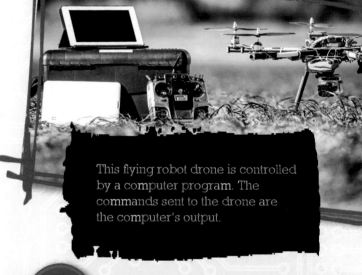

This flying robot drone is controlled by a computer program. The commands sent to the drone are the computer's output.

Your wish is my command

Robots and remote-controlled machines are also output devices controlled by a computer. Robots are used in factories, for example, to do jobs usually performed by humans. An example of a remote-controlled machine is an unmanned aerial vehicle (UAV), which is an aeroplane that can fly without a pilot.

Sounds Amazing

Early computers were silent or only made beeping noises. Today's computers can be noisy machines, playing music and blasting out sound effects from games.

⬇ Computer sound

Sounds are caused by vibrations that travel through the air as waves. These sound waves can be gathered in by a microphone, which turns them into electrical signals. A **sound card** or sound processing chip inside a computer can convert these electrical signals into computer data by turning lots of little samples of the sound into numbers. This data is stored as a **sound file**.

⬇ Sound shaping

Once stored on a computer, the sounds can be replayed or they can be edited and changed using computer programs. Sound files can also be transferred between computers or loaded into the memory of a portable music player or smartphone.

When a sound file is played, it's turned back into electrical signals that are sent to a loudspeaker. These signals make the cone of the loudspeaker move back and forth, moving the air to create sound waves.

A smartphone or music player may play sounds quietly. You can place them in a dock with bigger speakers and an electronic device called an amplifier to increase the loudness of the sound.

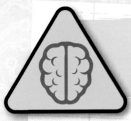
Make Some Noise!
Here are three challenges involving sound.
See how many of them you can complete!

1. Sounds on the Move
A mobile phone contains a microphone and most
also have a sound recording program. Record
some sounds on a phone while you are out and
then play them back when you get home.

http://tinyurl.com/chngsound

2. Sing High, Sing Low
See how sounds can change note
from high to low using a computer
connected to the Internet. Ask an
adult to help you type the address
on the left into a browser and have
some fun playing with sound.

3. Sounds Like Fun
Use a computer connected to the
Internet to learn more about sound
by visiting this web page full of
different experiments and activities.

http://tinyurl.com/learnsounds

TRUE STORY

Mega Memories Some music
players have enough
memory to store 40,000
songs. That's enough to
play a new song a day
for 109 years!

Picture Perfect

Cameras used to store images on film. You couldn't see the pictures until they were processed with chemicals and printed out as photographs. Today, digital cameras display pictures on screen in an instant.

Digital cameras

Digital cameras use a special chip that turns light collected by the camera's lens into electrical signals. The camera processes the electrical signals into computer data so that your picture can be stored as an **image file.** You can then look at the picture on screen, print it out or send it to another computer. The amount of detail a digital camera can capture is called **resolution**, which is measured in megapixels (millions of **pixels**).

TRUE STORY

Snap Happy Today, people take millions of photographs using digicams or cameras built into phones or tablets. Around 350 million digital photos are added to the social network site Facebook every day. That's an awful lot of photos!

Have some fun taking a 'selfie' on a smartphone.

STRETCH YOURSELF

Shrink Your Friend

Use a digital camera or smartphone camera with two friends to take a fun optical illusion image.

Get one friend to stand a few paces away and stick out a hand. Get the other friend to stand in the distance. Line them up so it looks as if a small person is standing on the hand. You will probably need to try this a few times to get it right.

What other optical illusion images can you take?

Digital video

Videos are just a series of individual pictures taken really quickly one after another. When played back, they show a moving scene. Small, tough digital video cameras can be mounted on a motorbike or skateboarding helmet to take amazing action videos.

COMPUTER Hero!

Steve Sasson built the first digital camera in 1975. It weighed over 3.6kg and took 23 seconds to store one tiny black-and-white photograph on a cassette tape. Each picture had a resolution of just 0.01 megapixels. Today's cameras offer 1,000 times greater resolution.

Computer Gaming

Hundreds of millions of computer games are sold every year. Some games are played on smartphones and tablets. Others are played on personal computers or special gaming computers called consoles.

Many gaming joysticks have 'hot' buttons that you can program to do certain jobs in different games.

 Game controls

Some games use the computer's keyboard, mouse or touchscreen to provide the playing controls. Other games, particularly action games, need special controllers. These controllers (or input devices) might be a joystick or gamepad and let users change direction quickly in the game.

Some gamers use controllers such as this racing car steering wheel which mimics the controls of a real car.

Motion sensing

Computer games using motion controllers let players make realistic movements such as swinging a racquet in a tennis game. Most motion controllers are hand-held. As the player moves the motion controller around in the air, the game copies the movements and commands on the screen.

Kinect for the Xbox 360 games console does away with hand controllers. Instead, sensors detect the player's body movements as they jump or aim a kick, for example. The console then converts these into realistic movements in the game.

Mario, the hero of Super Mario Bros.

COMPUTER Hero!

Shigeru Miyamoto thought about being a manga comic artist before becoming a games designer at Nintendo. He developed Super Mario Bros., the Legend of Zelda and other smash hits. He also helped develop Wii Fit and Wii Sports — the best-selling console game of all time.

TRUE STORY

Minecraft Madness In 2014, the government of Denmark recreated its entire country in the computer game Minecraft to get kids interested in the nation and its geography.

27

MEGA and Mini Machines

Some computers are faster than others. The fastest and most powerful are called supercomputers. These giant machines have thousands of processors all working together. Other computers can be as tiny as a stamp.

⬇ **Supercomputers**

Supercomputers are often used to make a **simulation** of complicated things such as weather patterns to work out what will happen next. One of the largest supercomputers – the Titan supercomputer – is kept in 200 large cabinets. It works thousands of times faster than a desktop computer. In 2013, the Tianhe-2 supercomputer became the fastest computer in the world. It can make 33 thousand million million calculations every second!

An example of a supercomputer

Mini computers

There are also small hobby computers such as the Raspberry Pi. This has a processor, memory and USB ports so that you can connect it to a keyboard and screen. The Raspberry Pi is only the size of a credit card, but Intel's Edison computer is even smaller. It is only the size of a postage stamp and will one day power wearable computers in clothes.

American computer engineer **Seymour Cray** is regarded as the father of supercomputers. His first computer, the CDC 6600 in 1963, could make 9 million calculations every second. His 1976 Cray-1 supercomputer was 20 times faster. Both were the fastest computers in the world at the time of their launch.

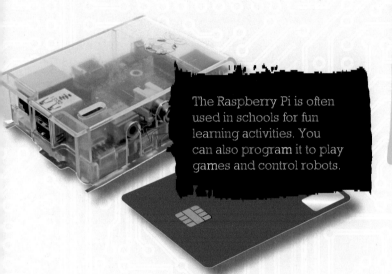

The Raspberry Pi is often used in schools for fun learning activities. You can also program it to play games and control robots.

Cray-1

STRETCH YOURSELF

Design a Wearable Computer
Can you work out how to design your own wearable computer?

Here are some questions to ask yourself:

☞ How will it be powered?

☞ Where will you put the display?

☞ How would the user control the computer?

Glossary

binary A number system containing only ones and zeros.

byte A small unit of memory that can hold up to eight binary digits (ones and zeros).

circuit A path along which an electric signal can be carried.

CPU (Central Processing Unit) A powerful series of electronic circuits that perform all the calculations in a computer and also control the machine's other parts.

cursor A moving symbol such as an arrow or flashing block, which shows a position on a computer's screen.

e-book A type of computer file containing all the text and images of a book, which is accessible by a computer.

heatsink A device that cools some types of silicon chip by carrying heat away from them.

image file A type of computer file that holds a photograph or illustration.

inkjet A type of printer that uses ink forced out of tiny holes, called jets, to print.

motherboard A printed electrical circuit board containing key parts of a computer and with connections for other circuit boards to join.

operating system The computer programs that run a computer's basic functions and manage other programs running on the system.

peripherals Devices such as printers, mice or keyboards that connect to a computer.

pixel Short for picture element, a pixel is a single point or dot, thousands or millions of which make up a digital image or a computer display such as a touchscreen.

programmed When a computer is given a set of instructions so that it works in a particular way.

RAM (Random Access Memory) A type of computer memory that can store information and be rewritten.

resolution The amount of detail that a digital camera can capture or a monitor screen can display. It is measured in megapixels (millions of pixels).

ROM (Read Only Memory): A type of permanent memory that doesn't lose data when the computer is switched off.

silicon chip An integrated circuit made up of thousands or millions of microscopic electronic parts etched onto a small wafer of silicon material.

simulation A computer program that acts as a model of a real-life event or system, such as a car crash or flying an aircraft.

sound card A set of circuits that enables a computer to produce sounds and often to record and change them as well.

sound file A type of computer file containing music, speech or other sounds which can be played on a device such as a tablet or iPod.

stylus A pencil-like object used as an input device on laptops and tablets that have touchscreens.

Further Resources

Books

Future Science Now: Communication by Tom Jackson (Wayland, 2014)

How Things Work: Electrical Gadgets by Ade Deane-Pratt (Wayland, 2013)

Technology Timelines: Digital Technology by Tom Jackson (Franklin Watts, 2015)

The World In Infographics: Technology by Jon Richards & Ed Simkins (Wayland, 2014)

Websites

http://www.computersciencelab.com/ComputerHistory/History.htm
A history of computing website with lots of pictures of exhibits.

http://www.explainthatstuff.com/how-computer-memory-works.html
A detailed explanation of how computer memory works written in clear English.

Answers

page 9 Find the Computer Port

a A port for plugging in a monitor.

b A port for connecting a USB mouse to a computer.

c A socket for connecting headphones to a computer.

Index